# THE NEW WORLD HELD PROMISE

*Why England Colonized North America*

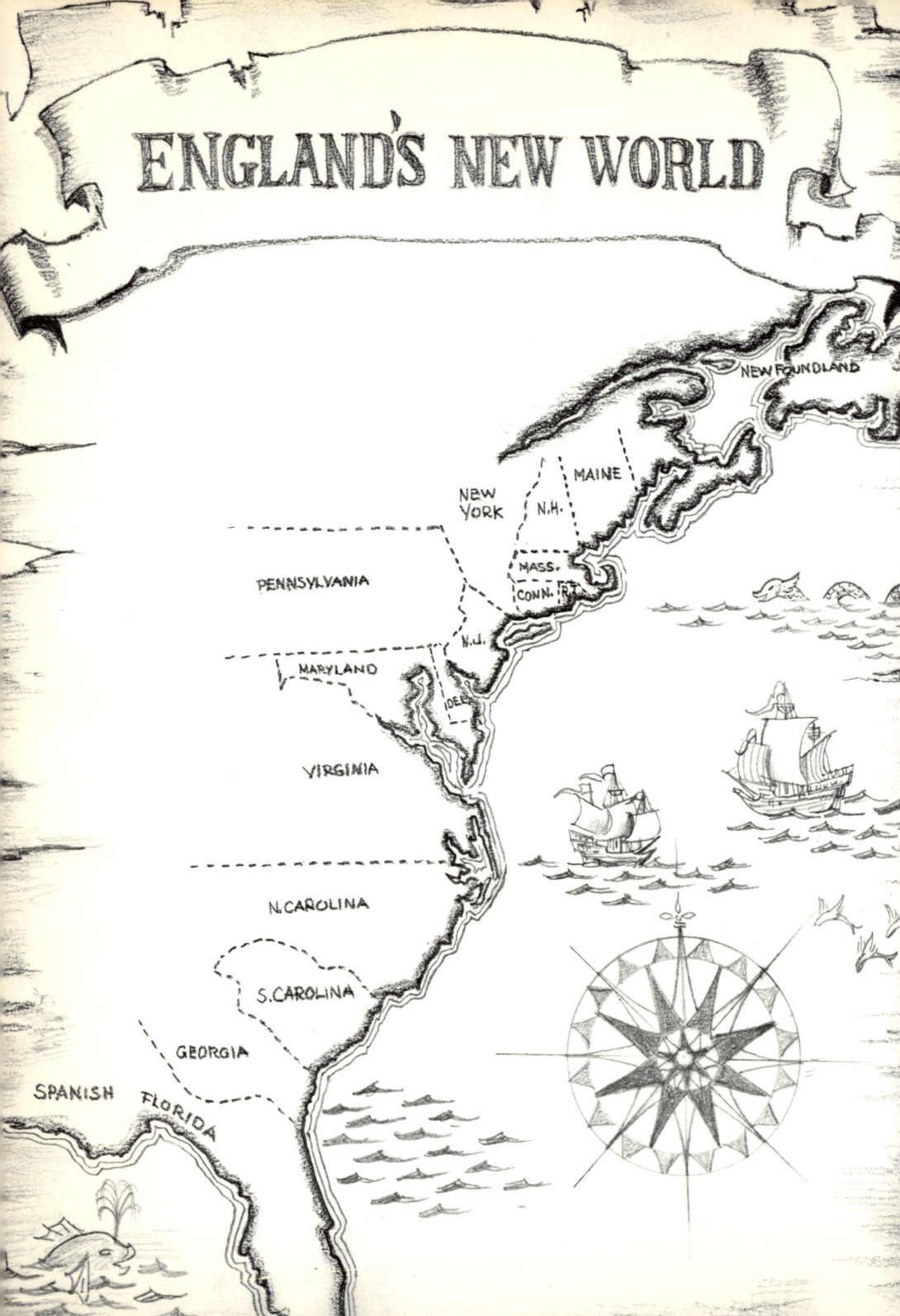

# THE NEW WORLD HELD PROMISE

*Why England Colonized North America*

by **NEIL GRANT**

Illustrated by Paul Frame

JULIAN MESSNER  NEW YORK

*Books by Neil Grant*

## THE NEW WORLD HELD PROMISE
Why England Colonized North America

## ENGLISH EXPLORERS OF NORTH AMERICA

Published by Julian Messner, a Division of Simon & Schuster, Inc. 1 West 39 Street, New York, N.Y. 10018. All rights reserved.

Copyright © 1974 by Neil Grant
Printed in the United States of America.

Design by Virginia M. Soulé

Library of Congress Cataloging in Publication Data
Grant, Neil.
    The New World held promise: Why England Colonized North America.
        SUMMARY: Examines the reasons for and process of English colonization of North America from the first attempt in Newfoundland to the founding of Georgia, the last colony.
        1. United States—History—Colonial period—Juvenile literature. [1. United States—History—Colonial period] I. Frame, Paul, illus. II. Title.
E188.G77 1974   973.2   73-20000
ISBN 0-671-32655-4
ISBN 0-671-32656-2 (lib. bdg.)

# CONTENTS

1 • THE FIRST ATTEMPT     8
       Sir Humphrey Gilbert
       Gilbert in Newfoundland

2 • RALEIGH AND VIRGINIA     18
       Raleigh's First Colony
       The Lost Colony

3 • VIRGINIA: THE ANSWER     30
    TO ENGLISH PROBLEMS

4 • THE VIRGINIA COMPANY     34
       Jamestown Founded
       Volunteers for Virginia

5 • PILGRIMS AND PURITANS     42
       The People of Scrooby
       The Pilgrims in Holland
       The *Mayflower* Sails

6 • THE BIRTH OF NEW ENGLAND     52
       King and Parliament
       The Massachusetts Bay Company
       The New England Colonies

7 • LORD BALTIMORE'S GREAT ESTATE     63
        Calvert Resigns
        The Maryland Charter

8 • THE GROWING EMPIRE     71
        The Reign of Charles II
        New York
        Carolina
        Pennsylvania

9 • THE "NOBLE DESIGN": GEORGIA     82
        James Oglethorpe
        Between Florida and Carolina
        The Georgia Trustees
        The Georgia Colonists

INDEX     93

# THE NEW WORLD HELD PROMISE

*Why England Colonized North America*

# THE FIRST ATTEMPT

When Christopher Columbus dropped anchor off a West Indian Island in 1492, he changed the history of the Western world. Until then, the people of Europe had not explored far beyond their own frontiers.

Columbus' discovery of America opened a whole new continent to Europe. Within a few years, Spanish ships were sailing back and forth across the Atlantic. Their holds were filled with the silver and gold that they had found in Mexico and Peru. Europeans had never before seen such treasure.

Other nations looked on enviously as Spain grew rich. When the French and the English set out on their own voyages of discovery, they found that Spain had taken all the richest territory. Besides, the Spaniards claimed that *all* the New World belonged to them. Other nations were told to keep away.

England did not accept the Spanish claim. In time of war—and sometimes in peacetime too—English captains attacked the Spanish ships, and captured the American treasure that they carried.

At first, Spain was not much worried by its English rivals. England was a small farming country, not a great world power like Spain. But in the sixteenth century, trade with other countries was becoming more important in England than farming. The rulers of England worked hard to build up trade and their navy.

Merchants became important men. In London, Bristol, and other English ports, the merchants built grand houses for themselves and hired fleets of ships to carry their goods to foreign markets. The shipyards were busy, building new and better ships for the growing trade.

Although Englishmen were interested in trade, they were slow to understand the part that colonies could play as centers of trade. Then, in the reign of Queen Elizabeth I (1558-1603), they began to look further ahead. For the first time, books, plays, and poems were written about the New World, and some writers said that England should have colonies there. Many reasons were suggested. Spain had found gold and silver in the New World. England might discover mines just as rich in parts where the Spaniards had not settled. Other products

—rare spices that did not grow in Europe—might flourish in the land across the ocean.

At the same time, England's rivalry with Spain grew more bitter. Among the West Indian islands, in the Caribbean Sea, English pirates hunted Spanish ships. They raided coastal towns in the Spanish colonies, and the Spaniards sent their best warships—great wooden vessels like floating castles—to drive the English off.

The Spaniards had bases in their colonies where they could repair their damaged ships. But English ships had to sail all the way back across the Atlantic to reach a friendly harbor. Here was another reason for English colonies in the New World.

Besides trade and the navy, and the rivalry with Spain, there was another reason why England began to expand overseas in the reign of Elizabeth I.

The Elizabethan age was a time of nationalism, when men were proud to be Englishmen. A hundred years before, a small farmer in the country, or a craftsman in a town, had hardly thought of England as a nation. He had looked no farther than the border of his county or province. But in Elizabeth's reign, such a man was glad to say that he was a subject of the Queen of England.

*As England's rivalry with Spain on the high seas increased, she realized she would need friendly harbors in the New World.*

This was the age, too, of fine English musicians and artists. It was the age of Shakespeare, the greatest poet in the English language, who roused the spirits of his countrymen with his lively plays about English history. In every part of life, in music and theater, business and trade, England was expanding. Englishmen believed that they belonged to the greatest nation in the world, and they said so—loudly.

## SIR HUMPHREY GILBERT

The first Englishman to make a serious effort at colonization in North America was a courtier named Sir Humphrey Gilbert. In 1578, the Queen granted him a patent to found a colony in what is now Newfoundland (Canada).

A patent is a license awarded by the government. It gives to one man (or one company) the sole right to carry on a certain kind of business. If a man invents a new kind of machine, he "patents" it to prevent others from copying it. Sir Humphrey Gilbert's patent, signed by Queen Elizabeth I, gave him the right to make a settlement of Englishmen on any land not ruled by a Christian king.

Sir Humphrey was well known at court as a keen colonizer. He had written a book about his ideas for a settlement in the New World. He believed that colonies in North America would bring more trade to England. And, like other explorers of the time, he hoped to find a sea route through the new continent, which would lead him to rich markets in China and Japan, lands that English merchants never visited.

But Sir Humphrey was interested in other things besides trade and making money. He was an adventurer, always ready to take a risk, always eager for bold acts and new ideas. If he were alive today, he would surely be interested in space travel.

He was, perhaps, a little too eager for new adventures. Although he knew almost nothing about the land on the far side of the Atlantic, he had written a long book describing it! He was certain his colony would be a great success, but his plans were vague and he had little money for such an expensive project.

In fact, his first attempt to found a colony in Newfoundland met with disaster even before it got started. His little fleet was scattered by a storm when it had hardly lost sight of the English coast. Sir Humphrey took refuge in an Irish port, and another ship, captained by his half-brother, Walter Raleigh, reached mid-Atlantic before he had to turn back.

Gilbert had spent all his fortune on his first expedition. His patent was to last for six years only, but by 1583, the last full year before it ran out, his colony existed only in his mind. Where was he to find the money to try again?

Help came from his half-brother. Walter Raleigh was a handsome, intelligent, and ambitious young man who had risen in the world since he captained a ship in Gilbert's first expedition. Queen Elizabeth liked him, and there was no quicker way for a man to get rich in Elizabeth's England than by gaining the favor of the Queen. Raleigh had received large estates, and had become rich enough to invest money and ships in Gilbert's second expedition to Newfoundland.

*Sir Humphrey Gilbert claimed Newfoundland for the Queen of England.*

## GILBERT IN NEWFOUNDLAND

No colonies yet existed anywhere in North America, except in Spanish Florida. But the coast of Newfoundland was well known to Europeans. Fishermen from many countries sailed there every year to hunt the great shoals of codfish. They had built a few huts near the shore, where they dried their catch. During the summer, some of them lived in Newfoundland for weeks at a time.

Late in July of 1583, Sir Humphrey Gilbert proudly led his four ships into the harbor of St. John's. Unfor-

tunately, his ship got stuck on a rock, and the fishermen had to pull it clear. They were not pleased when Sir Humphrey announced that he was now governor of the region and all the fishermen would have to pay a tax.

The new governor next decided that a grand ceremony was needed to mark the beginning of his rule. It was rather difficult to put on a grand show in this wild country, which was thousands of miles from civilization. Still, he did his best. Solemnly he cut a piece of turf from the ground, and a branch from a tree. Holding turf in one hand and branch in the other, he announced, in the name of the Queen of England, that all the land for six hundred miles around belonged to him.

Many of the fishermen looking on were not Englishmen, but Frenchmen, Dutchmen, and Scandinavians. Why should they accept Sir Humphrey's claim? Yet no one raised a protest.

Sir Humphrey took his ships exploring along the coast, but bad luck still followed him. Sailing too close to the shore, his largest ship struck an unseen reef. In a moment, the sea spun the ship around and the rocks tore open her hull. The crew were drowned, and all the supplies, maps, and tools were lost.

This last disaster was too much even for the eager Sir Humphrey Gilbert. Sadly, he gave the order to return to England.

Five ships had set out from England, but only two,

16

the *Golden Hind* and the *Squirrel,* were left. Gilbert himself sailed in the little *Squirrel.* She was a tiny ship for an ocean crossing—no bigger than a modern lifeboat.

The captain of the *Golden Hind* begged Gilbert to come on board the larger ship, but he refused. He had sailed on the *Squirrel* until then. To change ships would look like cowardice. He would not desert the *Squirrel*'s crew.

In mid-Atlantic, they ran into a storm. As night fell, the waves grew angry. They rose higher and higher, until the captain of the *Golden Hind* could hardly see the little *Squirrel.*

Sir Humphrey Gilbert sat in the stern of his ship. A lantern swung above his head, and by its flickering light he was reading a prayer book. When the two ships drew close together, he called out cheerfully to the men on the *Golden Hind,* "Remember, we are as near heaven by sea as on land!"

About midnight, the lights of the *Squirrel* suddenly disappeared. On the *Golden Hind* the captain strained his eyes against the darkness. Then the melancholy cry of the watchman crushed all hope. "Cast away! "Cast away! The General is cast away!" The *Squirrel* had gone to the bottom of the ocean, carrying with her Sir Humphrey Gilbert and all his hopes for a colony in the New World.

# RALEIGH AND VIRGINIA
## 2

Gilbert's death was a sad blow to his half-brother. "I have no true friends like him," the proud Raleigh lamented. But grief did not prevent him from taking up Gilbert's plans. He asked the Queen to renew Gilbert's patent in his own name, and Elizabeth willingly agreed.

Raleigh planned his colony more carefully. He decided that Newfoundland was too cold, and so he hired two ships to search for a better place, farther south. The Queen refused to let Raleigh risk his life on the voyage. He put a Captain Barlow in charge of the expedition, while he waited impatiently at home.

After four months, the two ships returned safely to England, and Barlow rushed to tell Raleigh his news.

The ships had sailed first to the West Indies, then

followed the coast north until they came to some island off what is now North Carolina. Choosing an island called Wococon, Captain Barlow landed on the sandy beach. He looked around suspiciously, but all was quiet and peaceful.

Raleigh's first question was, "Is the land fertile?" One look had showed Captain Barlow that it was. Vines, thick with ripening grapes, tumbled down to the shore, some even trailing in the sea. Everywhere he looked— along the shore, in the hills and plains, even up in the tall cedar trees—he saw fat bunches of grapes.

"What about meat?" Captain Barlow had the answer to that, too. He ordered one of his men to fire off a gun, and great flocks of crane rose into the air, making a noise like an army of men all shouting at once. Colonists could dine on roasted crane, and on the fish that swarmed in the sea.

On the nearby island of Roanoke, Captain Barlow had visited a friendly Indian village. He traded pots and pans for furs, and admired the Indians' maize. "Their corn is very white," he reported to Raleigh "and very good-tasting."

"A perfect paradise." That, said Barlow, was a fair summing-up of the country. Raleigh named it Virginia, in honor of Elizabeth, the Virgin Queen.

Raleigh wanted to hear only good news, and his captains knew they would get no thanks for saying the

19

*Captain Barlow's description of Wococon and Roanoke convinced Raleigh that it would be a good place to establish a colony.*

country was not fit for English settlement. They told Raleigh what he wanted to hear. It was not the whole truth.

For instance, what about the inhabitants? The Indians had welcomed them, said Barlow. "You could not find a more kind and loving people in the whole world." But would the Indians welcome a colony? What would they think of a large number of strangers who came, not as visitors like Raleigh's captains, but to live forever on their land? That was a question Raleigh did not ask.

Other important questions went unasked and unanswered. The captains had anchored their ships in the open sea, because they had not found a harbor in the islands. In calm weather, no harm had come to them. But what would happen in the stormy season, when hurricanes howled up from the south?

## RALEIGH'S FIRST COLONY

Raleigh's first colonists would soon find unpleasant answers to these questions. They set out, about one hundred of them in five ships, in 1585. They were a rough, hard-living band of men. Many had fought in England's wars, and they journeyed to America not to start a new life, but because they were doing a job. Raleigh was paying their wages. They were more like a military expedition than a group of colonists, and they took no women or children with them.

Their leader, Ralph Lane, a veteran of twenty years' fighting, was brave and quick-thinking, though rather quarrelsome. One of his assistants was Thomas Harriot, an able scientist and a friend of Raleigh's. Another was John White, an artist, who painted the first pictures of Virginia.

They soon discovered problems that Captain Barlow had not reported. As they tried to bring their ship in close to shore, they heard a grinding, rasping noise—the ship had grounded on a reef. They had to unload her and carry their supplies ashore in small boats.

Later, they found better shelter for ships off the island of Roanoke, and moved their settlement there.

Lane and his men spent more time exploring than planting seeds or building houses. None of them wanted to spend his life in Virginia (at that time "Virginia" meant the whole country from Maine to Florida). They wanted to find pearls, or a channel through the continent to the Pacific. "Make a quick fortune, then back to England and live like a king"—that was their idea.

Soon they were in trouble with the Indians. They

expected the Indians to give them corn, but the Indians had hardly enough corn for themselves. When Lane led a party to explore farther inland, he found that the Indians had run away from their villages, taking their precious corn with them. From village to village, the word had traveled: Beware the men with white faces and magic spears (guns) that kill from far away. Beware the white men who come to steal!

Weak with hunger, Lane's men had to kill two dogs that they had brought with them. They struggled back to Roanoke, with nothing to eat but dog stew flavored with sassafras leaves.

At their camp, Ralph Lane and Thomas Harriot talked about the chances for English colonies in Virginia. "This country is as rich as any in Europe," Lane said. "Crops can be grown, the seas are full of fish, and the hills with deer." He puffed at a pipe filled with the leaves of a strange plant that the Indians had given him.

An odd custom, Harriot thought, but quite pleasant. He did not suspect that one day a large and thriving colony would earn all its profit from growing this plant—tobacco.

"Yes, nature is generous in this new country," Lane went on. "But men will not come here to grow crops and eat fish. They can do that well enough in England. But if we should discover a rich mine, of silver, or of copper even . . ."

23

Harriot, a more intelligent man, looked further into the future. He put down the clock that he was mending, and shook his head.

"Men come to a strange land and hope to find riches. They expect to find gold and silver when they cannot even get enough food. That is foolishness. It will take time. Men must learn how to grow the native crops. They must bring horses and cattle from England to breed here. With all this good land, in time they will produce more food than they need. They will be able to sell food to England. Then they will grow rich, without the fabulous mines that they now dream of."

The future would prove Harriot right. But at that time, it seemed that the gloomy thoughts of Ralph Lane were nearer the truth.

The following summer, the English captain Francis Drake called at Roanoke on his way home from raiding the Spanish West Indies. He found Lane's men in poor spirits. The Indians had become their enemies, and they dared not move far from camp except in groups. They were short of food. The supply ship that Raleigh had promised to send was four months overdue.

The sight of Drake's ships, ready to sail back to England, made the men long for England. They asked Drake to take them home.

Just two days later, Raleigh's relief ship arrived, bringing supplies for the colonists. It found Roanoke deserted. The first Virginia colony had lasted only one year.

## THE LOST COLONY

Raleigh was disappointed by the return of Lane and his men, but he was not ready to give up. He had learned something from the failure of his first Virginia colony.

The next group of English people whom Raleigh sent out were real colonists, not men working for wages. Each man bought a share in the settlement, and received five hundred acres of land in return. There were seventeen women and ten children in the party, as well as about one hundred men. John White, the artist, was made governor. He was the only one among Ralph Lane's chief assistants who was willing to return to Virginia.

The colonists set out in 1587, but the voyage took many weeks. They had hoped to find a safe, deep harbor, north of Roanoke, somewhere on Chesapeake Bay. But when they came to Roanoke, they decided to stop there. Some of the houses built by Lane's men could still be used.

The colonists' greatest problem was lack of food. Because their voyage took so long, they had arrived too late to plant crops. Although they had guns (an early type of musket that was not very accurate), they were poor hunters. They had brought hardly enough food to get through the winter, and someone would have to return to England for more supplies. Since none of the others wanted to leave so soon, White agreed to go himself.

Before he left, he spoke to his little band of colonists. He warned them to keep guard against the Indians. Some of the Indians on the nearby island of Croatan were friendly, but those on the mainland were not. "You may decide to leave this place," he said. "But if you go, write on a tree where you are going. If you are in distress, or being attacked, mark the tree with a cross."

As his boat pulled away, he looked back. Through the trees he could see the stockade that the colonists were building. The wall of thick tree trunks which surrounded their houses would stop any arrow. A few people were still waving from the beach. He could see his daughter there. She was holding his newborn granddaughter, the first English child to be born in America.

When White reached England, in November, 1587, he went at once to see Sir Walter Raleigh. White explained the difficulties of the colonists on Roanoke, and Raleigh promised to help. Ships were purchased, but England was preparing for war with Spain and they were taken over by the government. Every English ship was needed for defense.

The following spring, White managed to hire two small ships, and he loaded them with supplies for the colonists. But when the ships got out to sea, their crews decided to turn pirate and took over the ships. White managed to get back to England, but none of the supplies ever reached Virginia.

White pestered Raleigh and anyone else who could help the colonists in Virginia. But another two years passed before a new expedition was ready. Even then, White had to leave without some of the supplies he needed.

At last, in 1590, John White returned to Roanoke. With a party of sailors, he landed one evening as the sun was going down. In the fading light, he could see smoke rising from a fire beyond the trees. He decided to wait until morning before making his way to the settlement. However, one of the sailors played some old English tunes on a trumpet, to let the colonists know that friends had arrived.

In the morning they found the fire. It was a heap of leaves, set on fire by the sun. The houses were gone, and the colonists had vanished, although the stockade was still standing. On a tree near the gate, White found one word carved in the bark: CROATAN.

Hoping to find his people on nearby Croatan, White sailed to that island. But there was no sign of any settlement. The vines still grew along the shore, and the cranes rose lazily. Sad and puzzled, White gave up the search.

Nearly three years later, he returned to Virginia for the last time. Again he searched, but he found nothing. He never discovered what had happened to

*What happened to the Lost Colony of Roanoke? No one knows.*

his friends, his daughter, and his little granddaughter. Nor has anyone since. What happened to the Lost Colony of Roanoke will be a mystery forever.

# VIRGINIA: THE ANSWER TO ENGLISH PROBLEMS 3

Spain's armies were much larger and stronger than England's. But the English navy was one of the finest. It could prevent the Spaniards from landing their troops on English soil. And so the war with Spain was fought chiefly at sea.

Sir Francis Drake, a famous English admiral, believed he knew how the war should be fought. "Strike at the King of Spain in his empire across the ocean," said Drake. "There you can do him most hurt." In Caribbean waters, Drake's speedy ships attacked the Spanish galleons and raided the Spanish colonies.

To sail from England to the West Indies took four weeks or more. It was a long way to go to fight a battle. By the time the ships reached home again, they were often leaking, their sails were torn, and their ammunition and their food were gone. How much easier it would be to attack the Spanish colonies if the English also had colonies in America! Then captains like Drake could repair their ships and take on new supplies before they raided the Spanish empire. They could also find shelter in a safe harbor before the voyage home.

Here was one good reason why the English should have colonies in North America. "Find a fair harbor—a place that may be well defended," Sir Walter Raleigh had told his captains. His colony would have been a naval base, and it had to be safe from Spanish guns.

Though England had no colony yet, many accounts of Virginia had been written. Ralph Lane and Thomas Harriot had told of their experiences. Most English people had heard of the Roanoke colonists.

Some of those who had returned with Lane had nothing good to say of Virginia. Other men spoke of the value of such a colony. "There are too many people in England," they said. "The highways are crowded with beggars and tramps—men who cannot find work or do not want it. They could be sent to Virginia. Let them go where they may be useful."

Many Englishmen still did not see how colonies could be useful. Empire builders like Raleigh and writers like Richard Hakluyt (who wrote the history of early voyages to America) tried to explain.

31

*Some Englishmen felt that beggars and tramps should be sent to the Virginia colony where they could find work.*

Colonies would give shelter to English ships fighting the Spaniards. Perhaps even more important, they would help to increase England's trade. Products like timber and furs could be sent to England, where they were scarce, while the colonists would buy articles made in England—clothes, weapons, tools, and many other things. The Mother Country would benefit in two ways: by importing products that otherwise had to be bought from foreign countries, and by the sale of English products to the colonies.

English merchants hoped that colonies might produce goods more valuable than furs and timber. The Spaniards had found gold, silver, and pearls in Mexico and Peru. Perhaps Virginia had silver mines too.

Not all the reasons in favor of colonies were good ones. For instance, Englishmen still hoped to find a way to sail to China and Japan. Not knowing how wide the new continent was, they believed that one of the rivers or inlets in Virginia might carry their ships through to the Pacific. In the sixteenth century, goods from Asia reached Europe by a long route overland and passed through many hands on the way. A direct sea route would make this Eastern trade much cheaper.

So there were many reasons why England should have colonies in North America, although not all of the reasons were right.

The Englishmen of Queen Elizabeth's time could not look into the future. But they did not need to look ahead to find reasons for colonizing the New World. They looked at their own world, and saw American treasure filling the pockets of their Spanish enemies. They saw bands of unemployed men, who were a danger to the peace, roaming England's roads. They saw nations growing rich on trade, and reaching around the world in their search for new markets and products.

Virginia seemed to hold the answer to many of England's problems.

# THE VIRGINIA COMPANY 4

After the failure of his Roanoke colony, Sir Walter Raleigh lost interest in Virginia. But other Englishmen did not.

Captain Gosnold sailed there in 1602 with thirty colonists. But they returned after a few weeks, finding life in the wilderness harder than they had expected. Three years later, the Earl of Southampton sent ships to explore the North American coast. In these years, other English captains visited Virginia for one reason or another. On their return, they told of the good climate, the fertile soil, and the herds of deer they had seen.

In England, times were changing. The great Queen Elizabeth died in 1603, and a Scottish king, James I, now sat on the English throne. Almost the first thing that James did was to end the war with Spain. Warlike Englishmen like Sir Francis Drake sneered at this peace-loving king. Spain, they said, was still England's enemy. But whatever his subjects thought, James was right to make peace. In the future, any English colony in Virginia need not fear a Spanish attack.

Men were changing too. The days of adventurers like Raleigh were nearly over. Successful colonies could not be founded by one man. Running a colony was not an adventure; it was a business. When King James granted a new patent for the colonization of Virginia, he did not grant it to one man; he granted it to a business company, the Virginia Company of London.

The Virginia Company was governed by a council, appointed by the king. The members were rich businessmen who were willing to put their money into the company in the hope of profits in the future.

The Virginia Company of London intended to keep its colonists under strict orders. Captain Christopher Newport, an experienced sailor who was to lead the expedition, was to look for a river up which ships could sail, and find a place for a settlement along the river. It should not be too near the coast, where it might be attacked from the sea. No one could tell how long the peace with Spain might last.

Two thirds of the colonists would build a fort

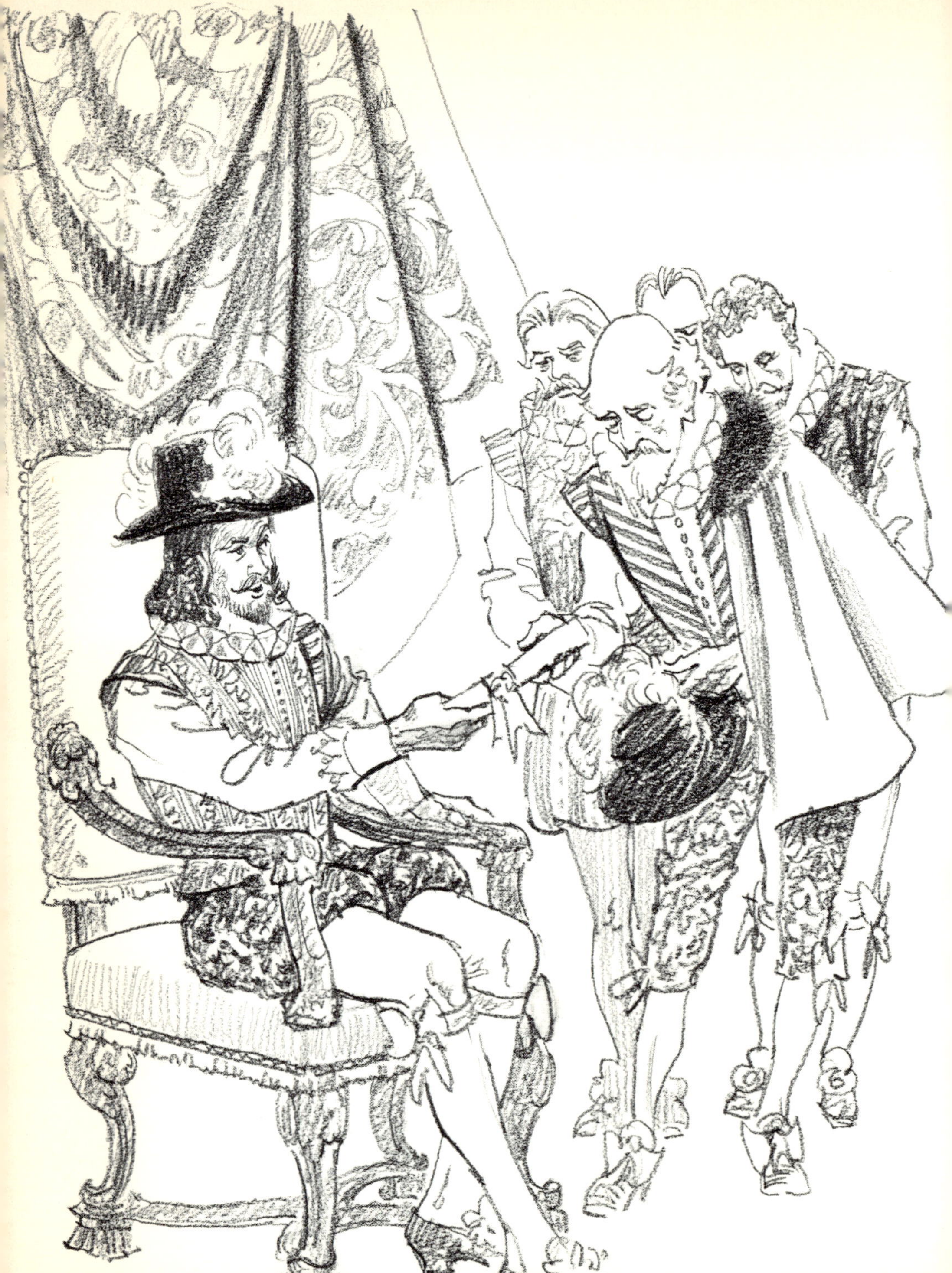

*Running a colony was no longer an adventure; it was a business. So King James granted the Virginia Company of London a patent for the colonization of Virginia.*

and prepare ground for farming. The rest would go with Captain Newport to explore farther inland. They would look for silver mines, and try to find a river leading toward the Pacific Ocean.

The company also gave orders for governing the colony and for carrying on trade. A church should be built where they would hold Church of England services. The colonists should try to make Christians of the Indians, and treat them with kindness and justice. When the colonists were settled, Captain Newport should return to England. The first party of colonists were all men. Women would follow later.

JAMESTOWN FOUNDED

On May 13, 1607, Captain Newport's three ships, battered after their long voyage, entered Chesapeake Bay and dropped anchor in the James River. Thankful to reach dry land, 104 men stepped ashore. After many failures, the English colonization of North America had begun.

The settlers called their little settlement Jamestown, in honor of the king. The place they chose was rather low and swampy. Mosquitoes buzzed through the

37

damp air. But Jamestown was surrounded on three sides by water, and it could be easily defended. Defense was more important than a good climate.

The early years were hard and dangerous. Most of the colonists just did not know how to stay alive in a wild country. They had to learn from experience, for no one could teach them.

They were not good hunters or farmers. For food they had only what they had brought with them and what they could buy from the nearby Algonquin Indian tribes. In bad times, a small amount of barley, soaked in water, was one day's food for five men. Every man had to stand guard one night in three for fear of an Indian attack. Weak from poor food and heavy work, many fell ill and died. By Christmas, 1607, less than half the first group of colonists were still alive.

The colonists did not work well together. Some were "gentlemen," who refused to do hard, rough work, like chopping down trees or building houses. As far as they were concerned, hard work was for servants. They had not done it in England, and they were not going to do it in Virginia! Men of that kind do not make good pioneers.

More colonists arrived, but many did not live long. In the winter of 1609-10, over four hundred people died, mostly from starvation.

Things were so bad that the colonists decided to

*The failure of the first Jamestown colony was due in part to the fact that not all colonists did their share of work.*

leave. They packed their belongings into their boats, leaving Jamestown to the forest and the Indians. But as they sailed down the river, they met an English ship arriving. On board was Lord de la War (for whom the state of Delaware was named). He had been sent out as governor of the colony, and he was not at all pleased to find his colony leaving. After a few tough words from the new governor, the colonists returned to the settlement and began again.

## VOLUNTEERS FOR VIRGINIA

The kind of men the Virginia Company wanted most were skilled craftsmen—carpenters, blacksmiths, wheelwrights, and others. Unfortunately, these men were not often willing to go to Virginia. A good craftsman could always find work in England. Why should he give up a good living at home to be a pioneer in the wilderness? The company could not pick and choose. It took almost anyone who agreed to go—ex-soldiers, poor laborers, restless adventurers, and men who could see no future for themselves in England.

Sometimes, servants of the Virginia Company went around the London inns, looking for likely men. When they found a man who seemed interested, they tried to persuade him to sign on as a settler. According to the company, Virginia was a "perfect paradise." There was gold lying about on the beaches, just waiting to be picked up. The Indians were the friendliest people in the world and treated the English like lords. The sun was always shining. The woods were full of deer and wild boar, and the fields were thick with corn.

Colonists who sailed to Virginia with their heads filled with these dreams had a shock when they arrived at Jamestown. They saw no gold lying on the shore, no pleasant fields, no herds of animals. They saw only a few huts, with weeds growing thick outside the walls.

There were only tired men in ragged clothes, carrying guns for fear of attack from Indians.

The merchants of the Virginia Company were losing hope of making a profit from their colony. In the first few years, all they gained were a few shiploads of timber and furs. It was hardly enough to pay for the supplies they sent out to Virginia.

But in the same year that Lord de la War arrived at Jamestown, a man called John Rolfe came to Virginia. He was to save the colony from poverty by growing a valuable crop, which could be sold in England at a high price. John Rolfe was Virginia's first successful tobacco planter. Tobacco—that "stinking weed," as King James called it—would save Virginia from ruin and make England rich.

# PILGRIMS AND PURITANS

## 5

In the sixteenth century, when Europeans began to explore other continents, great changes took place in Europe as well. At the beginning of the century, all Europe was Roman Catholic and obeyed the Pope as head of the Church. But by the end of the century, many countries had broken away from the Roman Catholic Church and had become Protestant.

In England, religion changed with every ruler—Catholic, Protestant, and then Catholic again. Finally, during the reign of Queen Elizabeth I, most people wanted a Protestant Church of England (although there were still many English Catholics too). But they did not agree on what kind of Protestantism they should have. Some wanted a Church ruled by bishops, like the Roman Catholic Church but without the Pope. Some wanted a very simple religion, with ministers chosen by the people. Catholics wanted to keep the old Roman religion, with the English Church ruled by the Pope.

Elizabeth and her government chose a middle way. The Church of England that they created was a Protestant Church, and the rule of the Pope in England was ended forever. But Elizabeth did not go too far with her Protestant reforms. The Church was still ruled by bishops, and many Roman Catholic customs were kept. The result was a Church of England halfway between Roman Catholicism and extreme Protestantism.

No government in sixteenth-century Europe believed in religious freedom. Every English man and woman had to be members of the Church of England, and anyone who refused could be arrested for treason. The Church was a state church: it was part of the government. In fact, the head of the Church and the head of state were the same person—the king or queen.

Elizabeth's religious compromise did not please everyone. Some of the people were loyal to Catholicism and to the Pope. They continued to worship, in secret, as Roman Catholics.

Others thought that Elizabeth's religious reforms did not go far enough. They wanted to sweep away everything that reminded them of the old religion. All the ceremony and mystery of the Roman Church should be abolished. Because they wanted to "purify" the Church of its Roman Catholic customs, these people were given the name Puritans.

The Puritans wanted to get back to the simple religion of the Bible. Religion should not be just for Sundays and church services, they said. It should be the rule of every man's life, from the moment he awakes in the morning until he goes to sleep at night.

Most Puritans wanted to remain members of the Church of England. Change it, yes. Reform it, certainly. But *leave* it? No.

But scattered about the country were a few small groups of people who had given up hope of "purifying" the Church of England. For them the English Church, with its ruling bishops, its priests in robes, its silver candles and carved crosses, was hardly different from the Catholic Church. They wanted freedom to worship in their own way, outside the established Church. Because they wanted to separate themselves from the Church of England, they were called Separatists.

## THE PEOPLE OF SCROOBY

One little group of Separatists lived near Scrooby, a farming town in eastern England. There were only about thirty of them when they first began to hold their meetings in 1606. They were tradesmen and small farmers, people whose families had lived among the flat fields and little villages around Scrooby for many years. They were not rich men or "gentlemen," but they were not poor laborers or beggars. All of them could read and write, though only one had been to a university. They were simple, ordinary folk, no different from most of their neighbors except for their religious beliefs.

Some, like seventeen-year-old William Bradford, had to walk miles from their homes to the house of William Brewster, in Scrooby, where they met. Brewster had been to Cambridge University and had been secretary to one of Queen Elizabeth's statesmen. With John Robinson, the minister, and young William Bradford, Brewster was to lead the Scrooby Separatists in the hard years ahead.

In a town of fewer than five hundred people, the meetings of the Separatists could not be kept secret. As William Bradford walked through the fields toward Scrooby, eyes watched from behind cottage windows. Other young men swore and jeered at him, and once a rock whistled past his head. In the muddy streets, the people of Scrooby muttered threats against the lawbreakers who defied the established Church.

Soon, government agents heard about the group in Scrooby. Five members of the congregation, Brewster among them, were ordered to appear before a Church

*As William Bradford walked through the fields toward Scrooby, he was threatened by the villagers for his religious beliefs.*

court, charged with "disobedience in the matter of religion." Brewster lost his job as postmaster of Scrooby, and the others were fined. Next time, they were warned, the punishment would be more severe.

They decided they would have to leave Scrooby and, to be really safe, they would have to leave England. Other Separatists had found safety across the North Sea in Holland, where they could practice their religion in freedom. One by one, those of the Scrooby group who could bear to leave their homes and everything they knew and loved slipped away to a port on England's east coast. No one was allowed to leave the country without permission, so they went secretly, not even saying good-bye to their friends.

They hired a ship and a captain to take them to Holland, but no sooner were they on board than the captain betrayed them to the government. They were dragged off the ship, their luggage was taken away, and they were sent home again.

The following year they tried again, this time in a Dutch ship. But less than half of them were on board when armed men appeared in the distance, riding hard toward them. The Dutch captain quickly hoisted sails and made for the open sea. But the women and children, and all the luggage, were left behind. Many months passed before they saw their husbands and fathers again.

**THE PILGRIMS IN HOLLAND**

Somehow in the next year or two, all the Pilgrims (the name that history has given the Separatists) managed to reach Holland. They settled in Leyden, a great university town and a rich port on the mouth of the Rhine River. The English government was still after them, but the governors of Leyden refused to drive them out.

In Leyden, the Pilgrims could worship at last in peace. But life was far from easy. They had to learn a new language and a new trade. Men who had lived in English farming villages now had to make their living in a foreign city. Yet some of them did well. William Bradford learned the cloth-making trade and, within a few years, he had bought a house and married a girl from another group of English exiles.

Under the wise leadership of John Robinson and

William Brewster the Scrooby Pilgrims lived in Leyden for ten years. Fewer than a hundred had come to Leyden in 1609, but six years later nearly three hundred men, women, and children gathered to listen to Robinson's sermons.

Still, the Pilgrims were not content. In a bustling, foreign city, they felt surrounded by sin and temptation. Their children grew up learning to speak Dutch and drifted away from the group. There were religious quarrels in Holland too, and a great religious war was boiling up in Europe. The Protestant Dutch were preparing to defend their independence against Roman Catholic Spain, the nation that claimed Holland as part of its empire. If the Dutch were defeated, the Pilgrims would be driven from Leyden. They decided to move on.

But where could they go? No country in Europe would welcome them. Anyway, they wanted to get away from Europe, away from the danger of war, away from the evils they felt were all around them.

## THE *MAYFLOWER* SAILS

The New World called them. America was a wild and dangerous place, but the Pilgrims were determined. "We doubt not but God will be with us, and if God be with us, who can be against us?" They would go.

The Pilgrims were poor. They could not afford to

buy supplies or to hire a ship and crew. Fortunately, merchants of the Virginia Company were looking for more colonists, and they agreed to provide the ship and supplies. In return, the Pilgrims promised to work for their living. They would send fish, furs, and other goods for the merchants to sell in England.

Even King James I, when he heard of it, approved the plan. He seemed to have forgotten, for a moment, his hatred of all Separatists. When he was told that the colonists hoped to earn their living by fishing, he only nodded and said, " 'Tis an honest trade. 'Twas the Apostles' own calling."

Preparations went slowly. A year passed, two years —sometimes the Pilgrims wondered if they would ever sail. By 1620, their agent in London was in despair. His arrangements were getting nowhere. "With so much coming and going, arguing and explaining," he wrote, "the summer will be past before we go." They would never reach America in time to plant crops before the winter.

When all was ready at last, they found that one of their ships was not fit to sail. That left only one small vessel, the *Mayflower,* to carry the Pilgrims across the ocean.

The *Mayflower* sailed on September 16, 1620. She carried 103 colonists, though only forty of them were members of the congregation at Leyden. The others, with John Robinson in charge, waited to join them once the colony was safely begun.

Not one of the 103 men, women, and children, crossing the Atlantic in a small wooden ship, knew what kind of place they were going to. The Pilgrims had lived all their lives in the towns and villages of England and Holland. They were going to a country with no houses, no shops, no roads, and no horses or cattle. No friendly inn would welcome them, no friendly voices greet them, and no church bells call them to prayer. They brought with them only a few simple tools, food supplies for a month or so, and cloth and metal goods to trade with the Indians. Could they live in the wilderness with so little? They did not know. But they had something far more valuable to them. They had their faith in God: "We doubt not but God will be with us."

They landed in Cape Cod Bay in November. After exploring the area, they began to build their little town. The colony of New Plymouth had begun.

# THE BIRTH OF NEW ENGLAND

## 6

The first years of the Plymouth colony were a struggle. Sometimes the Pilgrims could hardly remember what it felt like to be warm or well fed. Many of them died, and many became sick. At one time only seven people in the whole colony were strong enough to work. But the Pilgrims did not lose heart. As William Brewster said, "We are not like other men, who are discouraged by small things and wish themselves at home again." The Pilgrims would stick it out.

Slowly, the little town grew larger. More Pilgrims came over from Leyden. There were marriages and births, and new arrivals from England and Virginia. Some came too from other settlements in New England, which had been started after New Plymouth. Most of these settlements failed, but not all. The future states of Maine and New Hampshire grew from two of them.

Ten years after the arrival of the Pilgrims, the number of English people living in all New England would not have filled one town in the mother country. But in 1629 the King of England granted a charter to a group of men who called themselves the "Governor and Company of Massachusetts Bay," and thousands of colonists began pouring into Massachusetts.

Who were these people, and why did they decide to leave England in the 1630s?

KING AND PARLIAMENT

Back in 1603, when James of Scotland became King James I of England, the English Puritans rejoiced. James had been brought up by the Scottish Presbyterians, and the Presbyterian Church in Scotland was just the kind of Church the Puritans wanted in England. They hoped that James would give England a Presbyterian Church. But they were soon disappointed. James was no Presbyterian. He hated the Scottish system and much preferred the Church of England.

When the Puritans wanted to abolish all bishops,

James would not listen to such a dangerous idea. "No bishop, no king!" he roared. He believed that rebellion against the Church was only one step away from rebellion against the government. Those who abolished bishops, he felt, would soon be abolishing kings!

King James's government began to arrest and imprison those who would not obey the Church of England. For Puritans, the future looked grim.

In the seventeenth century, quarrels about religion were also quarrels about government. The quarrel between the king and the Puritans was part of a larger quarrel between the king and parliament.

*For their rebellion against the Church of England, Puritans were arrested and imprisoned.*

Who was to rule England, king or parliament? A king, said James I, rules by "divine right"; he is king by the will of God. Parliament may not tell him how to rule; parliament should do what the king asks, no more and no less.

The leading members of parliament, many of whom were Puritans, did not agree. Parliament has rights of its own, they said. Parliament provides taxes for the government, and therefore parliament has a right to say how the money should be spent. The king cannot make changes in the government or in the Church — unless parliament agrees.

As time went by, the quarrel between King James and parliament grew sharper. When he died in 1625, the argument still had not been settled.

James was succeeded by his son Charles I. Like his father, King Charles believed in the divine right of kings; he would not agree that parliament had any right to take part in the government.

Under Charles, the Church of England became more Catholic—or "Popish," as the Puritans said in disgust. Charles married a Roman Catholic princess, and he helped the Catholic king of France against the Protestant rebels in his country. When parliament protested, Charles told the members that it was none of their business.

Parliament feared that Charles was making himself a dictator. The rights of Englishmen seemed to be in danger, while the Church grew more Popish every year.

In 1629, Charles decided that he would end the argument for good. He had tried giving in to some of parliament's demands, hoping to silence his opponents. Instead, parliament came up with new complaints. Charles's patience was at an end. He arrested some of the leaders and declared parliament dissolved. In the future, he declared, he would rule *without* parliament.

## THE MASSACHUSETTS BAY COMPANY

The worst fears of the Puritans seemed to be coming true. Charles would become a dictator, they would be arrested, and the Church of England would never be purified. Like the Pilgrims before them, many Puritans began to think of leaving England altogether.

In the same year that King Charles decided to rule without parliament, the Massachusetts Bay Company was founded. Like all colonial companies, it was first of all a business company. Its members hoped to make a profit from trade and fishing. But many of the leaders of the company were Puritans, and profit was not their only motive. They dreamed of building a "City of God" in the New World, a refuge for the "true religion," a reformed and purified Protestant Church.

The Pilgrims had also desired a purer religion, but in other ways Pilgrims and Puritans were not alike. The

Pilgrims were rather poor people—small farmers and craftsmen. But the Puritan leaders were wealthy men, and some of them held important posts in England. William Bradford, governor of Plymouth, had been a cloth worker in Leyden. But John Winthrop, who became the first governor of Massachusetts, was a wealthy landowner and an official who lived in a large house with many servants.

In normal times, a man like John Winthrop, a landowner and a family man, would never have left his estate. But these were not normal times. In England, Winthrop saw Puritan clergymen driven from their parishes, and the Church was drawing ever closer to the hated Catholic religion.

The Puritans believed that God would strike England with some terrible punishment for its evil ways. Their God was the God of the Old Testament, fierce and unforgiving. "If we stay here," Winthrop wrote, "some Plague will overtake us." When they read in the Bible about the Israelites in Egypt, the Puritans saw the Israelites as themselves—God's chosen people. Like the Israelites, they dreamed of a "promised land." But their promised land was not Israel; it was New England. "God hath chosen that country to plant his people in," Winthrop declared.

It was John Winthrop and his Puritan friends who gained control of the Massachusetts Bay Company, and Winthrop himself was elected governor of the Company.

Thus it was certain that Massachusetts would be a Puritan colony. Profit or no profit, religion would be more important in Massachusetts than codfish or beaver pelts.

Before 1629, all English colonies in America were controlled by business companies in England or by the royal government. The Jamestown colony was governed first by the Virginia Company in London and later by the king. The Pilgrims were under contract to the English merchants who had lent them money. But the Puritans did not want to be ruled from England. The leaders of the Company in London might not always agree with the colonists in Massachusetts. Or the king might take away the Company's charter. (That had happened to the Virginia Company). How could they guard against these dangers?

Someone hit upon the answer. The *whole company* would move to Massachusetts, taking the charter along too. The company and the colony would become one and the same thing. As governor of the company, Winthrop would also be governor of the colony. With its own charter and its own government, Massachusetts would be safe from interference. The king could not easily take away the charter if it were in Massachusetts.

During the winter of 1629, Winthrop and his friends were hard at work preparing for the voyage. At the port of Southampton, a small fleet began to gather: the *Arbella,* the *Talbot,* the *Ambrose,* the *Jewel,* the

*Whale,* the *Hopewell,* the *Success,* and the *Mayflower* (which had carried the Pilgrims to Plymouth ten years before). Forty cows, sixty horses, one hundred goats, as much grain as could be bought (a bad harvest had caused a shortage), furniture, clothes, tools, and weapons were loaded into the little wooden ships. In fact, it was too much cargo, for during the voyage some of it had to be thrown overboard to save the ships from sinking.

Not all the colonists were Puritans. Some were ordinary folk who had no quarrel with the Church of England. Some did not care much about religion of any kind. But the leaders—men like Winthrop, who were to govern the colony for the next thirty or forty years—were dedicated Puritans. They believed that they were sailing to New England in the service of God, to create a purer Church in the wilderness.

THE NEW ENGLAND COLONIES

They sailed in the spring of 1630—nearly a thousand men, women, and children, crowded into eleven ships led by Governor Winthrop in the *Arbella.* Six more ships followed later in the year, and still more the year after. Governor Winthrop guessed that, by 1634, 4,000 people were living along Massachusetts Bay. By 1642,

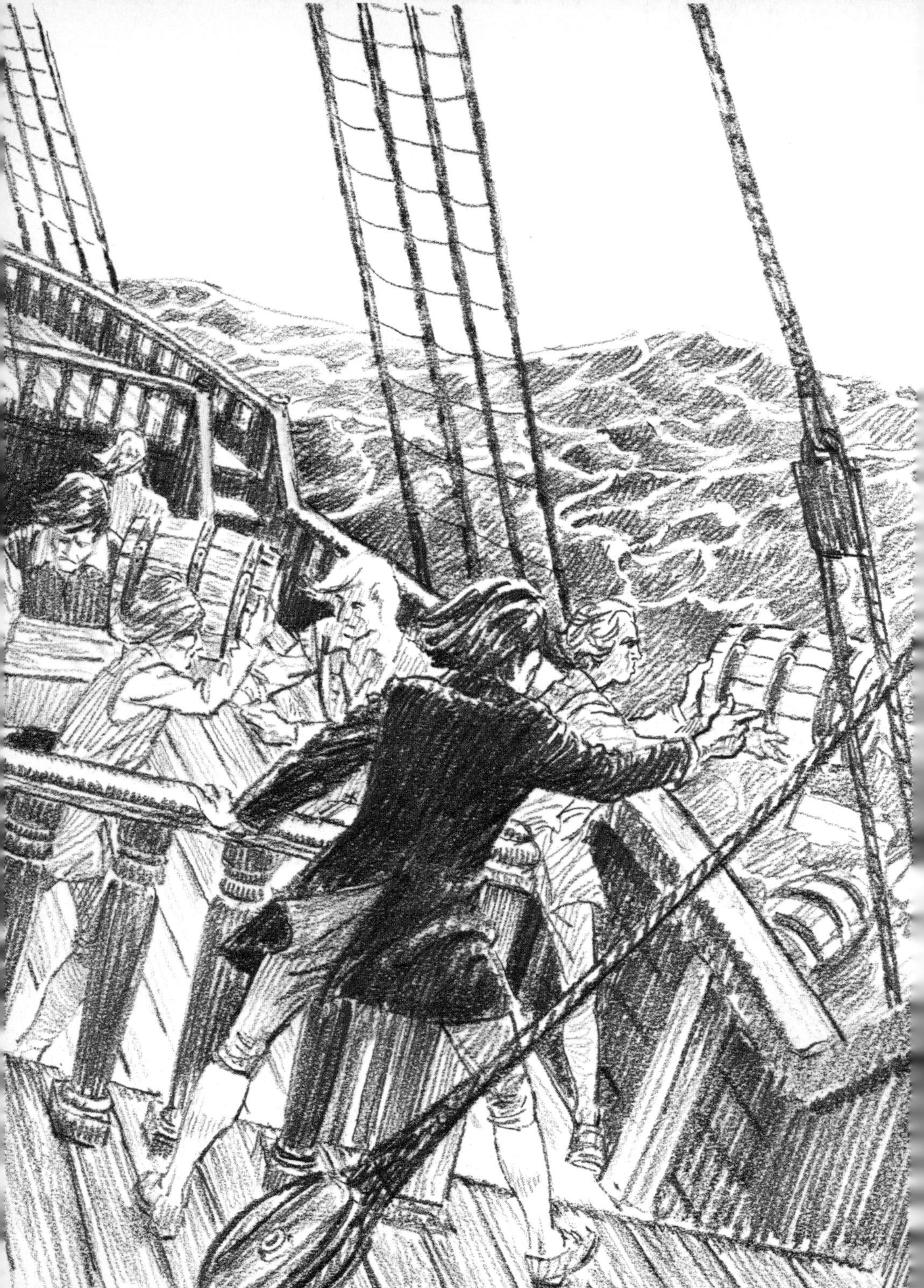

*To guard against interference from the king and businessmen, the whole Massachusetts Bay Company decided to move to Massachusetts. But their little ships were overloaded, and some of the cargo had to be thrown overboard.*

there were 20,000. The settlements grew: Salem, Dorchester, Boston, Watertown . . . From the northeast corner of Massachusetts, they began to spread out, north, south, and west.

The Puritans did not believe in freedom of religion, for everyone in Massachusetts had to obey the Puritan Church, just as everyone in England had to obey the Church of England. Those who would not accept the Puritan government had to leave. Some went back to England.

Others moved away from Massachusetts Bay and founded new settlements. One of these people was Roger Williams. Although he was a Puritan minister, he disliked the strict rule of the Massachusetts government. He moved to Plymouth for a time, but he did not fit in there either. Finally, he and a few friends founded a new town, which they called Providence. This was the beginning of Rhode Island.

Other little groups moved farther west and settled in New Haven and Hartford, from which the state of Connecticut would grow.

The Puritan settlement of Massachusetts was the

greatest colonizing effort ever made by the English people. At last, the dreams of Gilbert and Raleigh were coming true. For the people of Massachusetts were not traders, adventurers, and laborers, like the first Virginia colonists. They were not poor exiles, like the Pilgrims of Plymouth. They were English citizens of all kinds, wealthy gentlemen and poor servants, electing their own government and obeying their own laws. When Winthrop and his friends landed in Massachusetts, the history of a new nation really began.

# LORD BALTIMORE'S GREAT ESTATE

# 7

Before 1630, England's colonies in the New World were started either by one man or by a merchant company. After that year, however, the business of colonization passed once more into the hands of rich courtiers or friends of the king—men like George Calvert and William Penn.

George Calvert, the first Lord Baltimore, was the true founder of Maryland, although he died before the colony began. Calvert was the eldest son of an old English family. He entered the service of James I as a young man, and by 1618 he had risen to be chief secretary to the king.

He had also become interested in colonies. His wife came from a family of merchants who traded with

Virginia, and Calvert himself was a member of the Virginia Company. Not long after the Pilgrims arrived in Plymouth, he became the "proprietor" (owner) of a colony himself. The place he chose was not Virginia or New England, but Newfoundland (now part of Canada), where Sir Humphrey Gilbert had hoped to build a colony thirty years before.

As an important government official, Calvert could not leave England, but he kept in touch with his colony from London. The governor whom he appointed sent back good reports from Newfoundland. The land was fertile, the governor wrote, and the rivers full of fish; the wild animals were almost tame, and the sound of birdsong filled the air. There were even mermaids in the sea! Calvert was eager for good news, and he believed almost everything the governor wrote. But mermaids? Perhaps the governor's report was a little too good to be true.

One day, he would go and see for himself. Meanwhile, he was too busy with affairs of state. His government career was not going well.

## CALVERT RESIGNS

We have seen how King James I angered his Protestant subjects by seeming to favor Roman Catholics. James had ended the war with Catholic Spain, and he tried

*George Calvert, Lord Baltimore, received good reports from his governor in Newfoundland. But, were they really true? One day he would go to see for himself.*

to make the two countries friends by arranging a marriage between his son Charles and a Spanish princess.

Calvert helped to carry out James's policy. He believed in it, not only because he was the king's loyal servant but also because he was a Roman Catholic himself. For some time he kept his religion secret, but by 1623 most people at court knew that the king's chief secretary was a Catholic.

In that year Charles went to Spain to pay court to the Spanish princess. He soon returned—in a rage. He had been insulted, he said, by the Spaniards. It seems that the Spaniards never really wanted to marry their princess to a Protestant prince. Charles was a proud young man, and he had acted as though the Spanish princess were lucky to have the chance of marrying him. The Spanish did not like his behavior.

Back in England, Charles turned against his father's policy and swore he would not marry a Spaniard. King James, nearing the end of his life, was too weak to argue. The Spanish alliance was at an end.

As a strong supporter of the Spanish policy, Calvert was in a difficult position. Also, the "Popish" government was under attack from parliament, and the presence of a Catholic among the royal advisers gave the king's enemies another weapon to use against him. Calvert decided that he ought to resign, although Charles, who became king in 1625, asked him to stay.

The king made Calvert a baron and gave him some land in Ireland. Lord Baltimore (Calvert's new title) retired to his new estates. At last he had time to attend to the affairs of his Newfoundland colony. In spite of the governor's first reports, things were not going well. Lord Baltimore decided to take charge himself and, with his wife and children, he sailed to Newfoundland in 1627.

He soon made up his mind that Newfoundland was no place for a colony. From mid-October to mid-May, he wrote to the king, the place was a frozen waste. It might do as a fishing station, but as a colony it was useless. He asked Charles for permission to settle in Virginia instead.

Charles agreed, even though he felt that Lord Baltimore ought to come home. Baltimore too wanted to return to England, but he had others besides himself to consider. He had a duty to his family, his servants, and the forty or fifty people who had gone with him to Newfoundland. Most of them were Roman Catholics who,

*Lord Baltimore found that Newfoundland was no place for a colony.*

like the Pilgrims, hoped to find a home in the New World where they might worship in freedom. No Roman Catholic felt safe in England, even if he were, like Baltimore, a friend of the king.

Virginia was not the answer either. When Lord Baltimore arrived at Jamestown in 1629 with his little group of colonists, the Virginians gave him a cold welcome. They did not want Catholics living among them. They demanded that Baltimore take an oath that denied the authority of the Pope. That he would not do and, sadly, he sailed back to England.

## THE MARYLAND CHARTER

Despite the king's advice, Lord Baltimore was still determined to find a home for English Roman Catholics. When he arrived in England, he asked Charles to grant him land for a new colony, near Virginia but separate from it. The Virginians had not settled on the land north of the Potomac River. The king realized that Baltimore's mind was made up and agreed that he should have that region. Charles asked only that the colony be named for his queen, Henrietta Maria, and Lord Baltimore willingly agreed to the name Maryland.

The colony was much larger than the modern state of Maryland. It included what is now Delaware and parts of the future Pennsylvania and West Virginia. Lord Baltimore was to be the sole proprietor of the colony—the real ruler of Maryland, under the king. He could make laws, appoint judges, build towns and churches, and even wage war or make peace. In exchange for these great powers, he had to give the king one fifth of any gold or silver mined, and two Indian arrows—to be delivered every year to the royal castle of Windsor. The arrows were a symbol, to show that Lord Baltimore recognized the king as his ruler.

Unfortunately, Lord Baltimore did not live to see his charter stamped with the king's Great Seal. His work in Newfoundland, which had cost most of his fortune, had also made him ill. He died in 1632, and the name that appeared on the Maryland charter was the name of his son and heir, Cecil Calvert, second Lord Baltimore.

Cecil Calvert was only twenty-six years old when his father died, but he had worked closely with him while the charter was being prepared. He knew what problems lay ahead, and he was ready to spend all that was left of the family fortune on Maryland.

He set up an office in London, where he interviewed everyone who wanted to settle in his colony. If religious trouble was to be avoided, the colonists had to be selected with great care. Protestants as well as Catholics had to be chosen; otherwise his enemies could say that Maryland was nothing but a nest of dangerous Catholics. Many people hoped that the colony would be a failure. Virginia merchants feared that Maryland would be a dangerous rival, and they tried to have its charter cancelled.

In spite of such attempts to stop them, preparations were completed in less than two years. In the autumn of 1633, nearly two hundred colonists set sail for Maryland. The ships stopped at an island off the English coast, where two cloaked figures came on board. They were Catholic priests, traveling in secret, to escape the English authorities. They hoped to serve their God in greater freedom in the New World than England allowed.

Lord Baltimore sent his brother, Leonard Calvert, as Maryland's first governor. He could not go himself, since too many enemies in England were still working against his colony. He had to stay and fight for his rights. Many years later, he was still writing to his brother to say that he hoped to be free to leave England soon. When he died at the age of seventy, his eyes had never seen the rich tobacco fields and busy villages of Maryland.

# THE GROWING EMPIRE 8

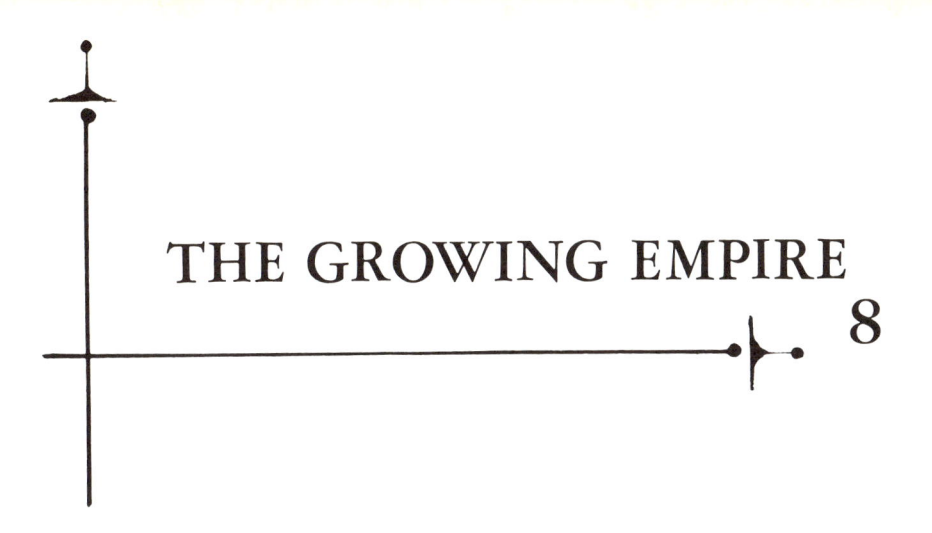

King Charles I managed to rule without parliament for eleven years. But by 1640 his government was bankrupt. and he desperately needed more money to deal with a Scottish rebellion. Only parliament could provide the extra taxes needed to pay for war. Charles had no choice: he called parliament.

The members arrived in London in an angry mood. They would not listen to the king's request for money, but loudy demanded changes in his government. Charles refused, and while an argument was still going on, he slipped out of London and began to raise an army. Parliament quickly gathered forces of its own, and civil war began.

At first, the royal armies did well, but gradually

parliament's forces gained the upper hand. The king's castles were captured, and his armies were defeated. Charles was taken prisoner, and put on trial as a traitor to his own country. In 1649, the king of England was executed in London, his own capital city.

Parliament's most successful general, Oliver Cromwell, took the title of Lord Protector, and for a few years he ruled as if he were king. Cromwell was a strong leader who was loved by his soldiers. He governed England well, but when he died, there was no one to take his place.

It looked as though civil war might break out again. But after twenty years of fighting and military rule, most people longed for safer, more peaceful times. Perhaps kings were not so bad after all, they thought.

The son of Charles I was living in exile in France, and ten years after his father's execution, his subjects invited him to return. In 1660, he entered London in triumph, cheered by the same crowds that had once cursed his father. He was crowned king as Charles II.

**THE REIGN OF CHARLES II**

During the troubled years between the outbreak of civil war and the return of Charles II, England did not

*Charles II returned to England in triumph and was crowned king.*

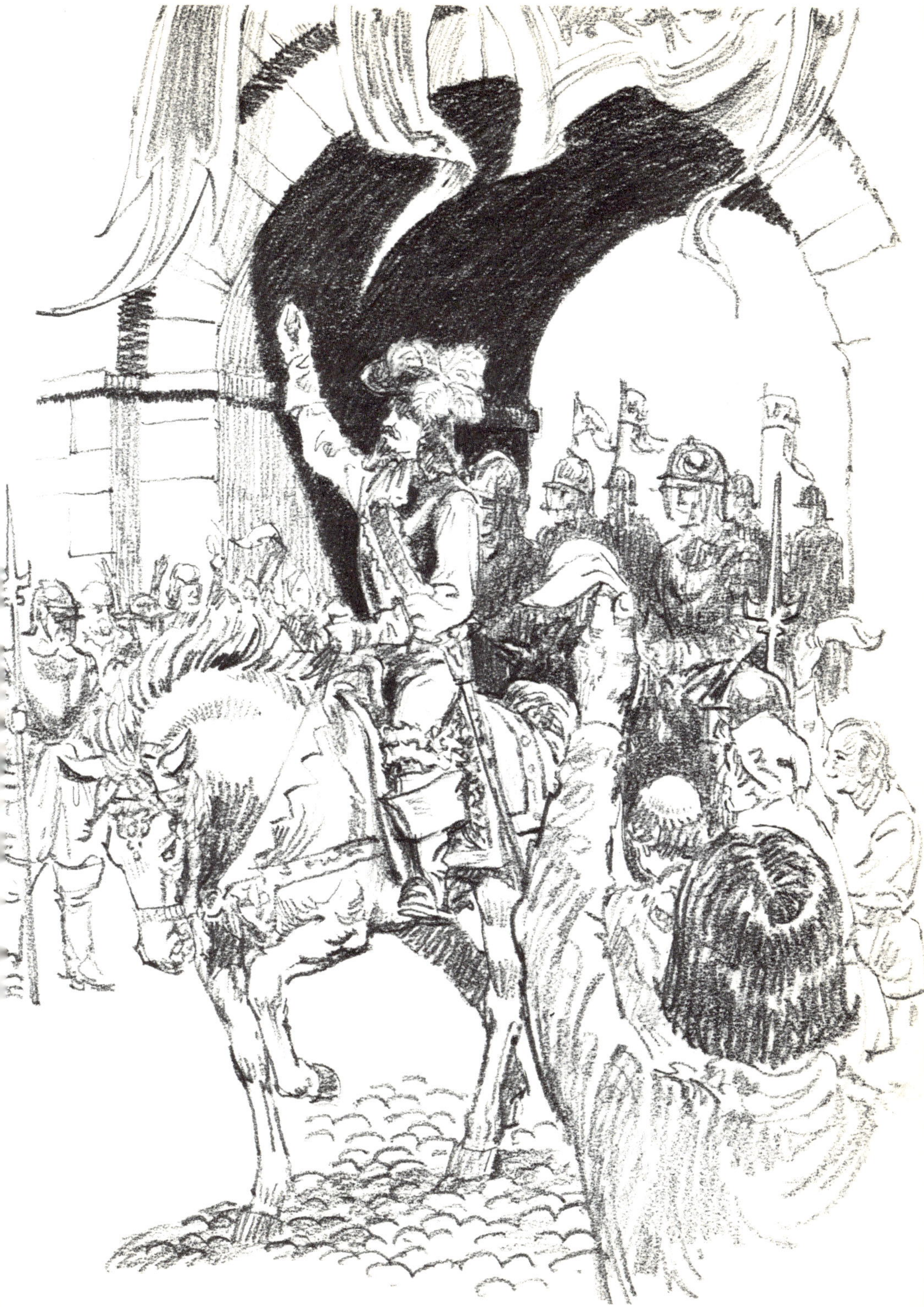

start any new colonies. Fewer ships crossed the Atlantic, and trade between England and the colonies began to suffer.

English merchants urged the new king to improve trade and build up the colonies. Charles promised to do all he could. With this support from the royal government, the English colonies expanded. The number of separate colonies, each with its own charter, more than doubled during Charles's reign (1660-85).

Each year, more villages were founded, and more forests cleared to make fields. New England was the fastest-growing region. In 1662, Connecticut was granted a royal charter, making it a separate colony. Rhode Island became one a year later.

But the largest additions to the English empire were three new territories: New York (including New Jersey), the Carolinas, and Pennsylvania. They were gained in different ways, and each one has its own history. But in one way they were all alike. All were "proprietorial" colonies, like Maryland. Each one became the property of a powerful landlord or a small group of landlords.

## NEW YORK

Trade, ships and colonies—these were the three pillars on which the power of England was based. Colonies provided goods that otherwise had to be bought from foreign countries. Colonial goods could also be sold to other European countries, while the colonists bought English-made goods from the mother country. And all this trade was carried on by English ships, earning more money for England and building up the English navy.

Of course, England was not the only European country whose strength came from trade and sea power. In the days of Sir Walter Raleigh, Spain had been England's chief rival, but the greatness of Spain was already passing when the first settlers arrived at Jamestown. In the seventeenth century, a new nation arose whose ships challenged the English in every ocean—the republic of the Netherlands.

The Dutch had settlements in North America, too. Between New England and Virginia lay the colony of New Netherland, stretching from western Connecticut and Long Island, through New York, New Jersey, and Delaware. Its capital, New Amsterdam, on the island of Manhattan, was a rich and bustling port. In the English colonies, Boston was its only rival.

But the Netherlands was a smaller country than England, and not many Dutch people wanted to emigrate. Since the government of New Netherland needed more colonists, they allowed the English to settle on its land. Surrounded by English colonies, and with many English settlers of its own, New Netherland was in a dangerous position. According to the English government, the Dutch were trespassers anyway. All the land from Maine to Virginia had been claimed by England.

When war broke out between England and the Dutch republic, the end was in sight for New Netherland. One morning in 1664, four English warships sailed into the harbor of New Amsterdam. Their commander aimed his guns at the houses of the Dutch merchants and demanded the surrender of the colony.

The Dutch governor, Peter Stuyvesant, was willing to make a fight of it. But he had no powder for his guns, his soldiers did not want to fight, and the citizens feared that their beautiful houses would be destroyed. Angrily, Governor Stuyvesant handed over New Netherland to the English.

Lord Baltimore argued that the captured territory rightly belonged to Maryland. New Englanders said it should be part of New England. But in the end, the

*One morning in 1664, English warships sailed into the harbor of New Amsterdam and aimed their guns at the Dutch colony, demanding its surrender.*

king gave it to his brother, the duke of York, and New Amsterdam was renamed New York in the duke's honor.

The duke thus found himself the ruler of a province larger than England. The southern part (New Jersey) he gave to a group of powerful English lords, keeping the northern part (New York) for himself.

## CAROLINA

In the Virginia charter of 1606, the region later known as Carolina was part of Virginia. No settlements were made there, however, and since Virginia had become a royal colony in 1624, the king was free to give the land away.

The founding of Carolina (it was not divided into North and South until 1694) was the work of eight men. All were men whom Charles II owed some kind of debt. One of them, Sir John Colleton, had helped the king while he was in exile. Another, Lord Clarendon, was his chief minister. A third, George Monck, had taken the lead in restoring Charles to the throne.

Charles could repay old favors easily by giving land in North America. It cost him nothing and, as new colonies meant more trade, he expected to profit along with the Carolina proprietors. Yet Charles was not entirely happy. The Carolina charter, granted in 1663, made the eight men "true and absolute Lords Proprietors," with the same wide powers that Lord Baltimore had in Maryland. It would be difficult for the government in England to control what happened in Carolina.

North, south, and east, the boundaries of Carolina were roughly the same as North and South Carolina today. But no boundary was marked in the west. The colony stretched right across the continent to the Pacific Ocean.

## PENNSYLVANIA

The government had begun to have strong doubts about giving colonies to powerful proprietors. Yet Carolina was not the last proprietory colony. In 1681, the king made a proprietory grant to William Penn. It covered the land between New York and Maryland, named "Pennsylvania" at Charles's suggestion.

Penn's charter described him as the "true and absolute Proprietor" (the same words as in the Carolina charter, eighteen years earlier), but it gave him fewer rights than the Carolina proprietors. For example, no laws could be passed, and no taxes imposed, in Pennsylvania without the agreement of the English government.

Still, Penn was lucky to get his colony. The king owed him a large sum of money, and the Pennsylvania grant was Charles's way of payment.

William Penn was the leader of a religious group

in England known as Quakers. The Quakers did not believe in a "Church" like the Church of England. Nor did they like the religion of the Puritans, with their sermons and Bible reading. They believed that God spoke directly to each person. Services, priests, churches, and all kinds of ceremony only got in the way of God's word; the Quakers would have none of them.

Most Quakers were peaceful folk, but a few of them stated their beliefs loudly and violently. They insulted those who disagreed with them, and they were not afraid of throwing a bottle at a passing priest to show their disapproval. The antics of these few earned the Quakers a bad name. In England, their meetings were forbidden, and thousands were imprisoned.

Like so many others before them, the Quakers hoped to find refuge in America. But none of the colonies would have them except Rhode Island, and they were not popular there either. They settled for a time in New Jersey, after the English had taken it from the Dutch, but they found no peace there. The only solution was to settle in a new colony, where the Quakers themselves would be in charge. And, thanks to the debt that Charles II owed to William Penn, the Quaker colony of Pennsylvania was founded.

The first colonists sailed in 1681, although Penn himself did not arrive until the following year. The colony was a success from the start. The Quakers were, on the whole, a more tolerant people than their enemies, who had driven them out of England. People of all religions, and all nations were welcome. Penn sold the land cheaply, for a penny an acre, and it proved to be good farming land. Merchants and craftsmen from other towns also settled in Penn's colony, and within a few years the chief town of Pennsylvania, Philadelphia, was the rival of New York and Boston.

# THE "NOBLE DESIGN": GEORGIA

## 9

In 1722, a man named Robert Castell was sent to the Fleet prison, in London. Like all prisons then, the Fleet was a horrible place. It was cold, wet, and stinking. The prisoners, as many as fifty men in one small cell, lay on stone floors while the dirt piled up around them. Prisoners who had money could rent a better room, and the warden grew rich. But those, like Robert Castell, who had no money, received the worst treatment. Castell was put in a cell with prisoners who had a dangerous disease, smallpox. He soon caught it himself, and in a few days he was dead.

Robert Castell was not a thief or a murderer. He was a quiet family man, the author of books about art, and he had never committed a serious crime in his life.

Why was he in prison? Because he owed money that he could not repay. For the "crime" of being in debt, he died in the Fleet, leaving his wife and small children without money or hope.

The case of Robert Castell was not unusual. London's prison were full of unlucky people who had been jailed for debts. Once in prison, they could not earn the money to pay the debt, and unless some friend or relative could help them, they remained in prison for months or years.

## JAMES OGLETHORPE

In 1729, these poor people found a friend and champion in James Edward Oglethorpe, a member of parliament. The state of prisons was a disgrace, said Oglethorpe, and the treatment of prisoners was cruel, stupid, and unjust.

Oglethorpe was a Londoner by birth. He joined the army when he was twenty-one and spent the next eight years fighting in Europe. But by 1718 all Europe was at peace, and Oglethorpe returned to England. At about the same time, his elder brother died, and he inherited the family estate.

For a man of action with his own fortune, politics was the best profession after soldiering, and Oglethorpe entered parliament in 1722. He became a critic of the government's foreign policy, and complained that nothing was being done to increase England's colonies.

Soon after this, Oglethorpe met Robert Castell. Although the two men were never close friends, Oglethorpe visited Castell in the Fleet, and was shocked by the dreadful conditions of the prison. Castell's death convinced him that something should be done and, as a member of parliament, he was the man to do it.

First, he talked privately to other members who were his friends. When he was sure that he had their strong support, he made a speech demanding an investigation of prison conditions. Parliament agreed, and set up the Prison Visiting Committee, with Oglethorpe as chairman.

Starting with the Fleet, the members of Oglethorpe's committee visited all the London prisons. They discovered enough horrible stories to fill a hundred books. Prisoners in chains, prisoners starved to death, prisoners tortured and robbed, women visitors attacked, and gifts of food stolen—there was more crime among the jailers than among the prisoners. The whole system was rotten.

Oglethorpe and his committee could not undo the

*James Oglethorpe visited Robert Castell in Fleet Prison. Out of this visit grew Oglethorpe's plan to send England's unlucky citizens to colonize Georgia, enlarging England's empire in North America.*

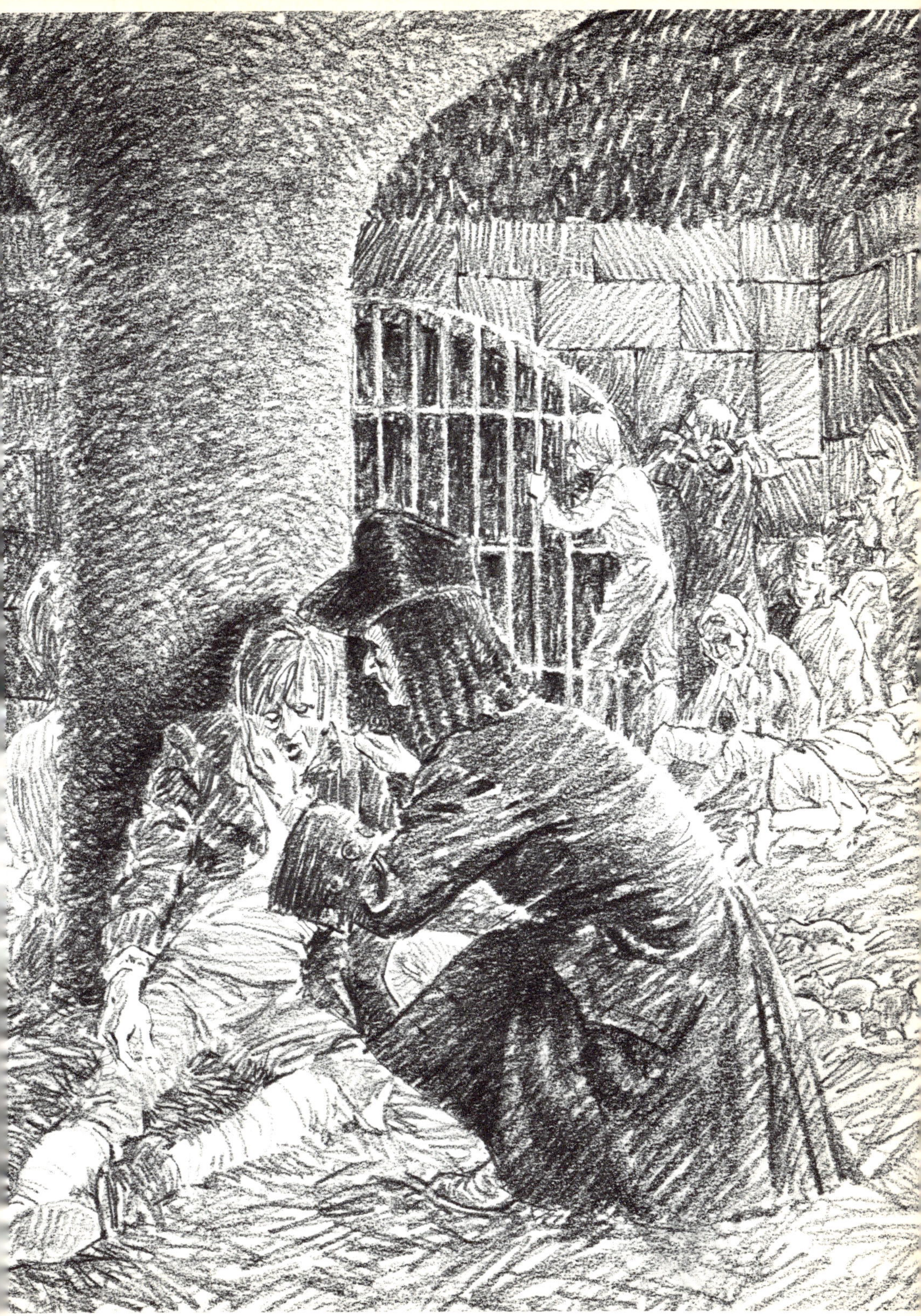

evil work of many years in a few months. But they made a start. Several prison wardens were arrested and tried, and over 10,000 people in prison for debt were given their freedom.

But what would happen to them after they had left the prisons? Oglethorpe realized that something more would have to be done, and not only for ex-convicts. Thousands of others lived in poverty, with no money, no property, and no jobs. Most people believed that if a man was poor, it was his own fault. But Oglethorpe felt that if the poor and hopeless could be given a start, they would be able to earn a decent living.

If England had no room for these people, there was still plenty of free land in North America. Here, said Oglethorpe, is a chance to accomplish two things at once. Small farms could be provided for thousands of England's unlucky citizens, and at the same time the English empire in North America could be enlarged and strengthened.

## BETWEEN FLORIDA AND CAROLINA

By 1730, when Oglethorpe was working out his plans, the English had occupied all the eastern coast from Maine to South Carolina. The French were in the north (Canada), and the Spaniards were in Florida. From north to south, the whole continent was occupied by

Europeans—except for one section. Between the Savannah and the Altamaha rivers there was a gap in the chain of colonies.

According to the Spaniards, this open region belonged to Florida. According to the English, it belonged to Carolina. But so long as no one actually lived there, neither side had a perfect claim.

The colonists in South Carolina wanted the English government to take possession of it. At least, they said, forts should be built to protect South Carolina from

*The Georgia colony was the last link in the chain of English colonies in North America.*

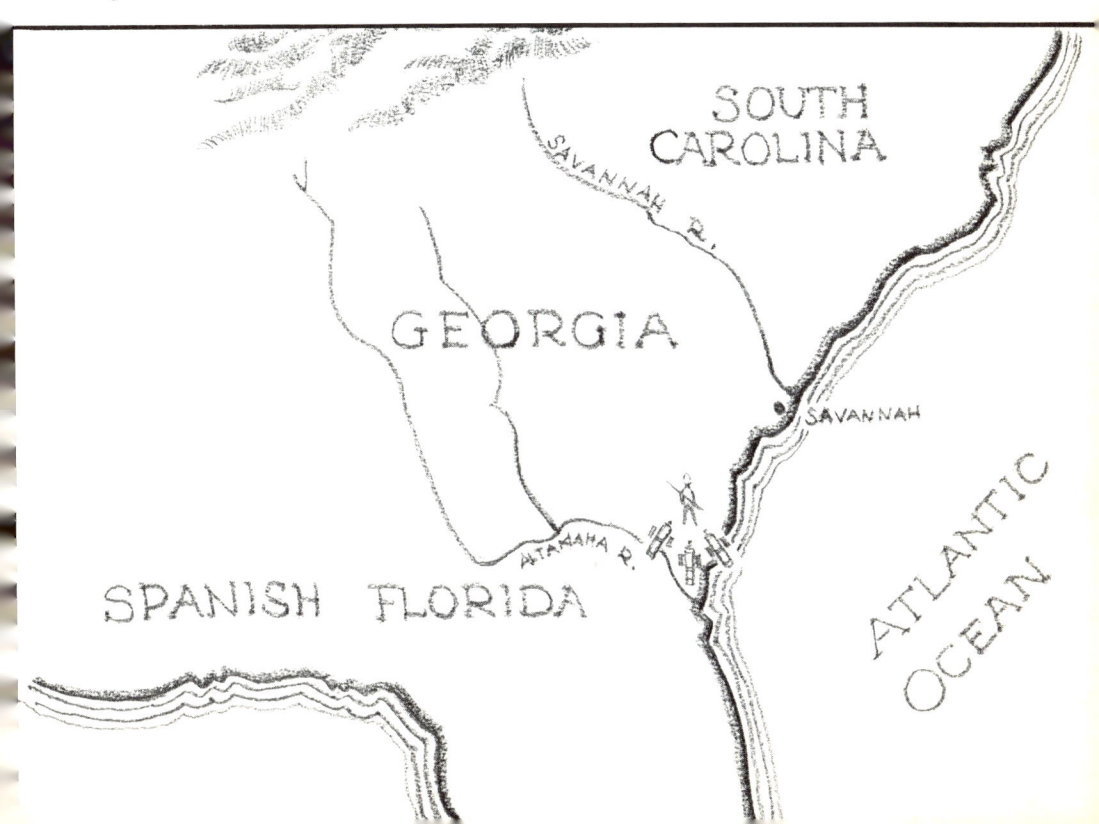

attack by Indians or Spaniards. One or two settlements were begun and, to the anger of the Spaniards, a fort was built on the Altamaha. But the settlements did not last, and the fort was soon abandoned.

Afraid of making Spain angry, the English government at first did nothing to help the Carolina colonists. But by 1730, after several Indian attacks and fights with the Spaniards, the government changed its policy. It agreed that the unoccupied region should be colonized.

So three things came together to make the colonization of Georgia possible. First, the English government decided to make good its claim to the territory. Second, the debtors released from prison, together with other poor and landless Englishmen, were willing to go there as colonists. Third, an able and energetic empire builder, James Oglethorpe, was ready to serve as leader of the colony.

THE GEORGIA TRUSTEES

Oglethorpe and twenty like-minded men—"Gentlemen of great Honor and Wealth," it was said—applied for a royal charter for a colony between the Savannah and Altamaha rivers. After many delays, the king, George II, granted their request, and the charter was signed and sealed in June, 1732. The colony was named Georgia in the king's honor.

The frontiers of the colony were different from the modern state of Georgia. From north to south, along the Atlantic, it was much shorter; but, like Carolina, it stretched right across the continent to the Pacific coast. This was a challenge to the French, who claimed the Mississippi valley and threatened to stop the English colonists from moving west.

Oglethorpe and his twenty colleagues were called the trustees of the colony. They were not powerful landlords, like Lord Baltimore or William Penn. They were forbidden to hold property in Georgia, and therefore could not expect to make any money from their trusteeship. Their power over the colony was limited too. Georgia was to remain in their charge for only twenty-one years. After that, the royal government would take over.

Having received their charter, the trustees' next task was to raise money. Parliament gave 10,000 pounds (worth over half a million dollars of today's money). The colonists of South Carolina gave another 2,000 pounds. The Bank of England gave some, and so did hundreds of private citizens. Not all the gifts were in money. Plants and seed, farm tools and clothing, guns and swords, and even barrels of beer and boxes of books were sent to help get the colony started.

Everyone in England who could read soon knew about Georgia. Newspapers and books were full of the project. Clergymen preached sermons about it. The trustees published advertisements, and one of them wrote a book to explain what a useful place the colony would be. Georgia, he said, would take thousands of poor people off the streets of England. It would be a refuge for European Protestants living in Catholic countries. It would provide silk, wine, and other products that England had always had to buy from foreign countries.

Like all those who wrote about the American colonies without visiting them, the writer was more enthusiastic than truthful. The air and soil of Georgia were so good, he wrote, that only a poet could describe their marvelous qualities. The climate was so healthy that Georgia Indians lived to be three hundred years old!

## THE GEORGIA COLONISTS

From thousands of people, all wanting to go to Georgia, the trustees selected a few hundred. They investigated each man carefully, choosing only "sober, industrious, and moral persons." They visited the prisons, looking for likely colonists among the debtors, but no one was allowed to go until he had paid his debts. Roman Catholics and Jews were not accepted. Poor but honest Protestants, skilled in some craft, had the best chance. Carpenters and blacksmiths, shipwrights and shoemakers—

craftsmen of all kinds—would be needed in Georgia. The trustees tried to pick men in every useful trade.

The lucky ones who were chosen received free passage to Georgia. They were promised fifty acres of land, as well as free tools and seed. No earlier colonists had been given such a good start. No wonder so many people applied for passage to Georgia.

The first colonists, with Oglethorpe as governor, sailed from England in November, 1732. They stopped first at Charleston, South Carolina, and then continued south. After asking permission to settle the land from the Yamacraw Indians, who lived in the area (something earlier colonists had not bothered to do), Oglethorpe began laying out the streets of Savannah in February of the following year.

The Georgia colony was not a great success, for plans drawn up in England did not always work out well in America. But it began with high hopes. A government official told the trustees that he believed "the design might prove a pattern for all future settlements."

No one knew that there would be no future settlements. Georgia was the thirteenth and the last of the English colonies in North America. Already, some colonists were resisting the efforts of the English government to rule them. The first rumblings of the American Revolution could be heard in Boston and Philadelphia. And

*After receiving permission from the Yamacraw Indians to settle their land, Oglethorpe began surveying and laying out the streets of Savannah.*

before he died, in London, at the age of eighty-eight, James Oglethorpe, founder of Georgia and its first governor, was to welcome the first ambassador of the United States to England.

# INDEX

## A

adventures, 62
Algonquin Indians, 38
Altamaha River, 87-88
*Ambrose,* the, 58
America. *See* North America
American Revolution, 91
*Arbella,* the, 58, 59
Asia, 33. *See also* China, Japan
Atlantic Ocean, 8, 10, 13, 16, 51, 74, 89

## B

Baltimore, Lord, 63-69
Bank of England, 89
Barlow, Captain, 18-22
beggars, 31
Bible, the, 44, 57
blacksmiths, 40, 90
boars, 40
Boston, 61, 75, 81, 91
Bradford, William, 45, 48, 57
Brewster, William, 45-46, 49, 52
Bristol, England, 9

## C

Calvert, Cecil, second Lord Baltimore, 69, 77
Calvert, George. *See* Baltimore, Lord
Calvert, Leonard, 70
Cambridge University, 45
Canada. *See* Newfoundland

Cape Cod Bay, 51
Caribbean Sea, 10, 30
Carolinas, 74, 78, 87-88, 89. *See also* North Carolina, South Carolina
carpenters, 40, 90
Castell, Robert, 82-84
Catholic. *See* Roman Catholic Church
cattle, 24
Charles I, 55-56, 65-68, 71-72
Charles II, 72-74, 78-80
Charleston, South Carolina, 91
charters, 58, 69, 88
Chesapeake Bay, 25, 37
China, 13, 33
Christians, 37
Christmas, 38
Church of England, 37, 42-44, 53-56, 59, 61, 80
Clarendon, Lord, 78
codfish, 14, 58
Colleton, Sir John, 78
colonies, English, 9-16, 21-23, 31-33, 58, 63
colonists, 19, 21, 24-27, 37-40, 50, 59, 68, 80, 91
colonization, 12, 35, 63
Columbus, Christopher, 8
Connecticut, 61, 74, 75
copper, 23
corn, 19, 23, 40
courtier, 12
Croatan, 26, 27

93

Cromwell, Oliver, Lord Protector, 72

**D**

debtors, 83, 86, 90
deer, 34, 40
de la War, Lord, 39, 41
Delaware, 39, 68, 75
Dorchester, 61
Drake, Sir Francis, 24, 30-31, 35
Dutch, 15, 48-49, 74-76

**E**

Elizabeth I, 9-12, 14, 18-19, 33, 34, 42-43, 45
Elizabethan age, 10
England, English, 8-9, 13-15, 21-26, 32, 34, 40, 46, 48, 51-52, 61-62, 74, 76; musicians and artists, 12; nationalism, 10; navy, 9-10, 30, 75; rivalry with Spain, 9-10; rulers, 9-15; ships, 32, 75; war with Holland, 76; war with Spain, 35, 64
Europe, Europeans, 8, 10, 14, 33, 42, 87
explorers, 13

**F**

farming, farmers, 37, 38
Fleet prison, 82-84
Florida, 14, 86, 87
France, French, 8, 15, 55, 86, 89
furs, 32, 33, 41, 50

**G**

galleons. *See* Spanish ships
Georgia, 82-92
George II, 88
Gilbert, Sir Humphrey, 12-18, 62-63
gold, 8-9, 24, 33, 40
*Golden Hind,* the, 15-17
Gosnold, Captain, 34

**H**

Hakluyt, Richard, 31
Harriot, Thomas, 22-24, 31
Hartford, Connecticut, 61
Henrietta Maria, Queen, 68
Holland, 47-48, 51, 75
*Hopewell,* the, 59
hunters, 38
hurricanes, 21

**I**

Indians, North American, 19, 21-24, 26, 37-41, 51, 88, 90
Ireland, Irish, 13
Israelites, 57

**J**

James I, 34-35, 41, 50, 53-55, 63-66
James River, 37
Jamestown, 37-41, 58, 68, 75
Japan, 13, 33
*Jewel,* the, 58
Jews, 90

**L**

laborers, 40, 62
Lane, Ralph, 22-24, 31
Leyden, Holland, 48-50, 52
license. *See* patent
London, England, 9, 64, 69, 71-72

Long Island, 75
Lost Colony, 25-29. *See also* Roanoke

## M

Maine, 53, 76, 86
maize. *See* corn
Manhattan, island of, 75
Maryland, 63-70, 74, 77, 79
Massachusetts Bay Company, 53, 56-58
Massachusetts Colony, 42-62
*Mayflower,* the, 49-50, 59
merchants, 9, 13, 33, 58, 63, 74
Mexico, 8, 33
Monck, George, 78
mosquitoes, 37
Mother Country. *See* England

## N

Netherlands, the. *See* Holland
New Amsterdam, 75-78
New England, 52-62, 74, 77
Newfoundland, 12-18, 63-66, 69, 86
New Hampshire, 53
New Haven, Connecticut, 61
New Jersey, 74-75, 78, 80
New Netherland, 75-77
New Plymouth. *See* Plymouth Colony
Newport, Captain Christopher, 35-37
New World. *See* North America
New York, 74-81

North America, 8-14, 17, 22, 30-34, 49, 56-58, 63, 68-70, 75, 78-80, 86, 90-91
North Carolina, 19, 78
North Sea, 46

## O

Oglethorpe, James Edward, 83-92

## P

Pacific Ocean, 22, 33, 37, 79, 89
parliament, 54-56, 66, 70, 72, 84
patent, 12-13, 18, 35
pearls, 22, 33
Penn, William, 63, 79-81, 89
Pennsylvania, 68, 74, 79-81
Peru, 8, 33
Philadelphia, Pennsylvania, 81, 91
Pilgrims, 42-53, 56-59, 62, 64, 68
pioneers, 38, 40
Plymouth Colony, 51-53, 59, 61-62, 64
Pope, the, 42-43, 68
Popish, 55-56, 66
Potomac River, 68
Presbyterians, 53
prisons, prisoners, 82-86, 90
Prison Visiting Committee, 84
proprietor, 64, 74, 79
Protestant, 42-43, 55-56, 64, 69, 90
Providence, Rhode Island, 61
Puritans, 44, 53-61, 80

## Q

Quakers, 80

95

## R

Raleigh, Sir Walter, 13-14, 18-27, 31, 33, 62, 75
religious freedom, 43-44, 47, 61, 68, 70
Rhine River, 48
Rhode Island, 61, 74, 80
Roanoke, 19-29, 31, 34
Robinson, John, 45, 48-50
Rolfe, John, 41
Roman Catholic Church, 42-44, 49, 55, 57, 64-69, 70, 90

## S

Salem, 61
Savannah, Georgia, 91
Savannah River, 87-88
Scandinavians, 15
Scotland, Scottish, 34, 71
Scrooby, England, 44-49
Separatists, 44-46. *See also* Pilgrims
Shakespeare, William, 12
shipwrights, 90
shoemakers, 90
silver, 8-9, 23-24, 33
smallpox, 82
soil, 34
soldiers, 40
Southampton, Earl of, 34
Southampton, England, 58
South Carolina, 78, 86-87, 89
space travel, 13
Spain, Spanish, 8-9, 26, 32-33, 49, 65-66, 87-88; army, 30; colonies, 30-31, 86; King of, 30; rivalry with England, 9-10

spices, 10
*Squirrel,* the, 15-17
St. John's, Newfoundland, 14
Stuyvesant, Peter, 76-77
*Success,* the, 59

## T

*Talbot,* the, 58
taxes, 15
timber, 32-33, 41
tobacco, 23, 41, 70
trade, 9-10, 13, 32-33, 37, 74-75
tramps, 31
trustees, 89-91

## U

United States, 92

## V

Virginia, 18-41, 52, 62, 64, 67-68, 70, 76, 78; climate of, 34; defense of, 38; gentlemen in, 38
Virginia Company of London, 34-41, 50, 58, 64

## W

Watertown, 61
West Indies, 8-10, 18, 24, 30
West Virginia, 68
*Whale,* the, 59
wheelwrights, 40
White, John, 22, 25-28
Williams, Roger, 61
Winthrop, John, 57-62
Wococon, 19

## Y

Yamacraw Indians, 91
York, Duke of, 78